CONNECTING CULTURES

CONNECTING CULTURES

Education as a Bridge in Relationships

AVERY NIGHTINGALE

Creative Quill Press

CONTENTS

CHAPTER 1

Introduction

This book will focus on our educational system and the importance of a multicultural education in a globalized society. In particular, we would like to stress the important role cultural definitions play as bridges or barriers in human relationships. In a globalized world, it is equally important to help children aim for the stars and, by example, contribute with benevolence towards greater transnational justice and solidarity. Democracy and human rights also contribute towards abolishing any vestiges of despotism and injustice wherever they may still exist. But one can hardly move forward with an attitude of brotherhood in a world in which cultural insensitivity and racism continue to be widespread.

We firmly believe in the power of educational institutions, particularly the school, and social institutions in general, as privileged spaces for the forming of personal identity, human relationships, and social cohesion. We know that we face the serious educational challenge of forming individuals who, by the force of an internalized and critical process, appreciate the importance of living with respect, trying to understand others who are different, and establishing cooperative and peaceful relationships. These are recognized as being the competences making up the personal content of the theoretical model on educated persons.

CHAPTER 2

The Importance of Education in Building Relationships

The importance of education is not only towards intercultural relationships but simple education also plays a crucial role in human life. The purpose of education is to produce a cultured person who can communicate well with other people, respect all different customs and traditions, and be a persuasive person who can interpret information received critically and share such information in a straightforward manner. They should also be able to fend off stranger things and criticism always with an open and critical attitude. Human life becomes more sophisticated with education, goals are achieved more easily, and the capacity to distinguish between right and wrong also grows. Each state in its Constitution provides for the establishment of formal education institutions, and the government also provides financial aid to parents through its subsidies, thus making it clear that their role in the effort to educate the public and improve life for the future. The old norm of a country passes away as the new norm of that country is passed on through the younger generation. After it is matured and accepted, then it is firmly rooted and becomes the tradition of the new country.

Bridging relationships through interactions or exchanges is not only applicable for intercultural relationships but can also be applied in our daily relationships with people around us. In earlier days, intercultural misconceptions often occurred due to the lack of interactions between the people of these conflicting cultures. Such misconceptions might lead to trust issues between members of different cultures as they do not have a deep understanding of each other. As traditions, foods, and beliefs of a certain cultural group are promoted, it is easy for members of other groups to misconceive and instead of sharing ideas and growing together, they instead isolate themselves from one another. According to Margaret Mead, an American cultural anthropologist, education is the method by which people conduct their socialization and where culture is intentionally passed on to the next generation.

CHAPTER 3

Cultural Exchange Programs

But it may feel frustrating that's apparently relying upon peculiar and nearly exclusive acquaintances. Nevertheless, although it may sound bizarre not you but the person has cultural exchange, how did the person think you got access to all of these writings, of these boring scientists if through the person? Wasn't the person part of the person's journey of multi-culture? And the person having taught me things, wouldn't the person owe then some capability for judgment? What came first, the academic writing or the social-cultural experience, coming and going with the person? Or is like de Chardin's pea, a "pseudo-problem", an ill-expression fixed with a turn of phrase?

Cultural exchange programs, which have been acknowledged as one efficient way to learn the culture, come in many shapes. From less formal ways like participating in an organization's events, doing voluntary work, living with a host family through Couch Surfing or being fluent in other languages, to more formal and prestigious programs like the ones sponsored by governments and prestigious organizations, only applicable to human sciences and law students, though indirectly but still in the exchange dynamic. However, it may look to you that's out of reach, lacking resources or the selection is elitist and therefore unfair, there is always the opportunity of waiting for a human sciences or law student to come around anywhere, like: a local university's study group, the trip guide at a local tour site, a similar exchange program for English students and less prestigious exchange programs that are very competitive or have odd requisites, like age, friend nationality and/or no report showing any diseases, already explained in the table titled General Data – Bachelor Graduation and Enrollments. And even if none of these situations ever happened, language may still make you able to make friends with the person.

CHAPTER 4

Language Learning as a Tool for Connection

Student instructors also create unique presentation opportunities within the context of the classroom, as they can give presentations about themselves and the culture. Rachelle Kenning, a second language learner of Japanese and Japanese class instructor, decided to improve her Japanese skills in high school, as well as her own cultural knowledge, in order to begin understanding native speakers in Japan. Currently, good communication between Japanese and herself is now a continuing language goal, and the most effective way to contribute to it is partly through her hands-on experiences in teacher training. In an attempt to step out of her comfort zone in terms of presentation style, she tried using English to Japanese sentence patterns, proper vocabularies, and less common grammatical points in her presentations. As a result, she not only won the Japanese presentation competition in 2016, but also concluded that gaining linguistic skills was achieved through continually embracing the challenge of public speaking. Expanding a different program with a wider variety of skills and preparing for JET in the next several years are her future goals.

Off-campus interaction with the greater community is as essential to language learning as engagement with other students in class. Eilya O'Brien, a 4th year Spanish major, has always wanted to fulfill the inclusion of the community in the educational purpose of her education by broadening her horizons beyond university borders. As an educator, her goal is to train others as well as herself and create a space that facilitates learning through communication with others in everyday settings.

Yueze Audrey Lai, Madison Bloomer, and Jennifer Balencia are the authors of the Daniel Jones Award 2018 article titled "Connecting Cultures: Education as a Bridge in Relationships." The article is a case study of two language students' experiences with not only becoming instructors in their respective language programs, but also in creating spaces that work to foster continued interaction and communication between students, as well as between the student instructors and South Lake's diverse communities.

CHAPTER 5

Promoting Diversity and Inclusion in Education

Diversity and inclusion are principles through which the right to learn, to teach, and to rule is to be realized. It is essential to subordinate everyone to the domain of culture, critical appropriation of reality, and transformation of the world to make them aware of the condition and possibility of domination of others and of themselves. The right to culture presupposes the awareness of diversity accompanied by the experience of dialogue that leads all to the language, to the disciplines, to the instruments, and to the expressions of art, to the sports competitions, to the games, to the solemn acts, to the fleeting meetings, and to the daily tasks through which men and women reveal to others and to themselves what they know, think, feel, and do, for what reasons and reasons.

Philosophers and theorists agree that school should promote justice, equity, autonomy, education, equality, fraternity, and cooperation. Nevertheless, how much are these political alternatives taken seriously and practiced at school? Among the main challenges of globalization is to promote an education that favors the formation of subjects, cultures, social groups, organizations, entrepreneurs, institutions, and states capable of responding to the immense challenges of justice, equity, autonomy, education, equality, fraternity, and cooperation between peoples and nations. Thus, it is essential to distinguish the principles from the political-pedagogical practices that appropriate, interpret, and adjust them to the historical conditions in which they were formulated.

CHAPTER 6

Breaking Stereotypes through Education

Through my personal encounter with the US education in computer science that has made me have a changed orientation culturewise, I got encouraged to influence students by passing on the same education to US middle and high school students. My desire is to facilitate the students to leverage computer science in debugging their orientation about other cultures. In the computer science they are learning, I am helping the students to see that there is more than one approach to solving a problem. Again, I am challenging the students to appreciate that it is irrelevant to assume that people from some cultures, because of their seeming underdeveloped technology in their country, may not be able or disciplined to solve similar problems in their domain. Through the education, the students see that they have an equal or competing capacity in creativity or other aspects of life. In mentoring the students, it is my intention to lay a strong foundation for their career as the assets to the future community by helping them to respect and appreciate that there are various groups of people on the earth. Through their career, they can maintain a valuable relationship with their community and also people from other countries by tapping into multiple approaches to solving problems in computer science and life.

Having lived in Nigeria for 18 years, I have been aware of some stereotypes people from the US have about Nigerians. From the US, I can remember observing those I meet from Nigeria to validate or invalidate the stereotypes. That experience allowed me to maintain interest in the stereotypical association of groups with culture. One reason I started mentoring US students was to let them appreciate other cultures and break down some of these stereotypes held against groups based on their culture. From the mentoring, it is evident that US students have poor attitudes about ethnic groups because of their cultural orientation.

CHAPTER 7

The Role of Technology in Connecting Cultures

Each country is characterized by its national tendencies, stereotypes, rituals, traditions, and prohibitions. A separate module for deciding whether to show a user a warning window or not was introduced in applications that take into account the calendar of religious Jewish holidays. Here we must not forget about the ritual color preferences by nationality or the occurrence of national Greek resistance images instead of the usual icons of various services. Companies tend to make their devices maximally personalized for each culture because web applications, games, everyday activities that a regular user does, he is doing through the devices. In almost every state, its own national holidays or establishments, whose dates are known to all local residents, are also celebrated.

Nowadays, technology has brought people closer than ever, and even the smallest smartphone can immerse any person in the diversity of cultural issues or simply initiate a conversation about some of them. In modern conditions, cross-cultural knowledge has become not just a guarantee of personal success, but also an urgent need to reduce distance and establish contacts. Successful devices and their design are made taking into account peculiarities, and for greater navigation, stereotypical symbols of different countries are used. This helps a person of any nationality to easily navigate in environments with elements of which he may not be familiar, also making contact with specialists in other fields. As an example, the American Globus LED, the Chinese smartphone product Le Fox, Samsung or LG from Korea, or the French car Citroen were considered.

CHAPTER 8

Building Global Networks through Education

To counter the imperialism of Western human rights advocacy, there is a need to develop a human rights issue related to international peace and security, beyond national security by itself. We are living in a global village. The United Nations declaration of the year 2000 as the International Year for the Culture of Peace is very relevant. The resolution has recommended investment in education for peace to transmit the philosophy of the project, to embrace peace in our lives. The contents of education for peace are simple. These include lower-level cognitive skills such as discrimination, prediction, retention, comprehending, and higher-level cognitive skills such as analysis, synthesis, and judgment. Giving educational content for peace is expensive because it is very complex. This is because we are living in a complex society. By giving content of universal peace, universal love, universal brotherhood, etc., our great saints and leaders like Sree Narayana Guru, Francis, and Abraham Lincoln have shown how man can become truly humane.

According to Tagore, "The highest education is that which does not merely give us information, but makes our life in harmony with all existence." It is high time that we convert our world of cultural diversity into a world of cultural understanding. In this direction, even if little steps are taken, perhaps it is possible for us to celebrate the unity in diversity. The challenge of diversity is becoming vivid in the light of human rights and conflicts too. The rhetoric of diversity, which has developed through human rights ethic, does not hold good in cases of recent inter-state conflicts, particularly in the case of the Gulf War and War in Yugoslavia, because in these cases, the North-South dialectics is very much explicit and immediate, and this is absent in the case of human rights advocacy.

CHAPTER 9

Empathy and Understanding in Cross-Cultural Education

A relationship can be deliberated significant if it gives its individuals a collective experience of life, history, society, and knowledge. Rahul, a high school art student in Nosara, hopes for a stable career after high school. He wishes to complete his studies so that he can further cultivate society through initiatives that help enhance knowledge around him. Rahul differently views creativity and freedom in the West as compared to Nosara. Growing up in a community where rural life revolves around beaches, monkey conservation, biodiversity, ecology, nutrition, surfing, sport fishing, and cooperative work, his definition of prosperity comes with a circumstantial definition. Furthermore, he explains Western countries' struggles that arise from commercialization, secularism, and socialism. Wine and crackers are conservative phenomena born of practical necessity: "Migrants do not ask much. The country that adopts them should appreciate workers because the richer a worker becomes, the richer the country gets."

According to Shreya, a former Indian student in the United States, empathy is crucial. A logical empathy encourages a more inclusive dialogue and intersections between cultures, unearthing a more impactful faith in one another, and using greater understanding. Bock and Khademian's interviews among international students and scholars reflect empathy as a critical sharing of cultures and knowledge to counter misunderstandings brought upon by stereotypes and discrimination. Schumann and Zander's study among students in international schools in Norway confirms that an educational community's shared atmosphere can be optimized with the practice of empathy. This study is applicable towards SchoolsUSA's goal to intentionally create an environment that promotes empathy. Understanding among different national citizens is possible through meaningful connections that emphasize similarities and minimize distinctions and variances.

CHAPTER 10

Education as a Means of Conflict Resolution

Education has a variety of goals, so it involves a broad variety of people's demands finally. The Open Education Declaration, United Nations, Human Rights Act, UNESCO, the Global Initiative to Address UNU Ethics and the Common Values, the Journal and Congress International Assembly, all have specific intentions, which are consciously related and typical of acknowledging and formally saying the value significance of education acknowledging and mentioning that education is the education and culture. Specifically, as required by the initiatives of these globally verified intercessors and others, for instance the precise article of definition in the column of the importance of open education, it must have a relationship with one or more topics formal informed explicitly by the explicit sentence.

Education is considered to be usually essential or good so as to be considered a human right and also as a significant element of human capital. It is an especial guide of various types of instruction and socialization. Examples include formal learning that occurs in a school setting, informal words, and also home teaching such as indigenous kyinker-nye and tight teachings and additionally the experience of developing that comes from yielding to several instructions and similar information and facts. It has been presented in several various methods as well as in all different things. In the classroom with other students of identical ages, these knowledges are typically taught by the staff or the teacher so that education can be instantaneous about something particular and also are usually motivated. Accordingly, people may receive a thorough education of a wide range of themes, often in formal settings, both in the individual and in the combined. The families could use different teaching techniques to education within a certain dedicated home.

CHAPTER 11

Education for Sustainable Development

On the other hand, education has also undergone a plethora of paradigmatic shifts. Rather, education beyond the conventional, regular subjects is not a contemporary invention. If defined as the tend-and-nurture activities, of which the term "Schooling" too is a modern coinage, it is but an entity that a substantial portion of the population has been exposed to in pursuit of their livelihood. Interest and ability are interrelatedness of the agents of learning, namely the student (child), teacher, and education. Fishing is a means of livelihood for a considerable percentage of the coastal population across the world. While ability can only come through the skill of learning that is taught in school, interest is a necessary but not a sufficient condition. The wealth of the so-called developed nations has been mainly generated from voluminous fish as much as natural resources and physical endowments, and not much of what we call development contributions were from the segments of the population that are classed as educated and skilled human resources.

Like the term "developing countries" and a number of others (holistic, empowerment, etc.), "sustainable" has many meanings in the arena of social action. While economic sustainability is one of the widely accepted meanings, the term has been used in combination with "rural development" and "community development" or "people's participation" in development. In 1970, Magson introduced "Sustainable Rural Development" as a model or operational model incorporating elements of "resettlement," "integrated community development," and "self-help," with less bias towards top-down, government-driven processes that were prominent during the time. It emphasizes self-reliance, mutual support, mutual respect among the poor through group activities, integration of employment, income-generating activities, skill development, and supplementary services, self-managed training and service delivery system, and entrepreneurship.

CHAPTER 12

The Impact of Education on Social Cohesion

Educational opportunities are fundamentally linked to a variety of social. There are key elements of social cohesion identified by Inglis. The first element is the goal of human well-being and sustainability of the biosphere. In this connection, educators may strive to endeavorly pursue equal access to all manners of human flourishing and to achieve justice in local arrangements that can lead to global justice. The second element is participatory solidarity, or new forms of human relations and sociality, that will produce a civil society in the life-world. There is what he calls a "humanizing of human relations and sociality which is an effect, as well as a condition, of social inclusion and political participation. We humans, for all we advocate the need for free or libertarian lifestyle, nonetheless crave for acceptance and recognition, something that can only truly be cherished within a community of friends.

This chapter has added to the bank of knowledge about education in promoting social cohesion not just in Indonesia, not just in the Philippines but to the extent possible, in other nation-states.

It is recognized that by its nature, social cohesion is a concept that is internal to the constitution of the communities and social structures. Thus, the concept perhaps has perceptual meanings which correspond to past, present and future events within the cultural and productive cyclic structure of communities. Due to its nature, social cohesion is not a process but perhaps more of a relational situation. This is because any increase or decrease in social cohesion can be directly observed via concrete and observable social relations. Not that it is less important for it may contribute to universality that enables a synergy at a global level. As the technological changes bring human's daily life into an interconnectivity in time and place, social cohesion should be empowered.

CHAPTER 13

Fostering Intercultural Competence in Education

There are a variety of models providing a valuable foundation in the development of educational concepts and strategies that promote intercultural competence, but not all educational approaches are effective. For example, those relying less on communication and virtual encounters, such as the "cultural effectiveness model," have lost their relevance even in the eyes of their developers and proponents. Intercultural competence in school cannot simply be taught, as emphasized by numerous publications and guidelines. Those members of the panel of experts studying the Educational Science Interpretation of Subject-Disciplinary Standards at the Universities in Hessen and Saxony noted the time-tested innovative designs and tried and tested successful basic elements of curricula that take into account the developmental, cultural, vocational, and occupational conditions of schoolchildren living within the economic cycles of globalization.

The question of whether there are approaches that advance the development of intercultural competence was addressed in a recent expert report presented to the German Ministry of Education and Research. The report and its recommendations draw on the practical results of the ten-year "Schools: Partners of the Future" exchange program (in short: "PASCH" schools) sponsored by the German government and the Goethe Institute. "The levels of awareness that young people achieve with regard to intercultural encounters are remarkable," notes Dr. Wolfgang Miersemann, who has managed the worldwide PASCH program at Goethe Institute's headquarters, during a meeting of experts that took place in Germany earlier this month. It has also become apparent, however, that there is no set formula for successful intercultural education. Throughout the country, it has become evident, adds Miersemann, that the structures of differently oriented cultures and systems of values must be learned about in a spirit of understanding and acceptance.

CHAPTER 14

Promoting Interfaith Dialogue through Education

This chapter aims to provide evidence in relation to the changing nature of the dialogue on faith and interfaith dialogue in societies that have witnessed a growing interdependence and lived within societies increasingly characterized by a multiplicity of faiths. It begins by explaining the terminology used in the context of interfaith dialogue. The chapter defines interfaith dialogue as the process of analyzing religious experiences through honesty, involving openness and a willingness to listen to the other. Establishing what interfaith dialogue is not is equally as important as defining it. The main misunderstanding made in reference to interfaith dialogue is the belief that it denotes the transposition of religious diversity into a synthetic whole, characterized by the indifference to the beliefs of another purer religious tradition. This misunderstanding proposes that interfaith dialogue is motivated by relativism. Interfaith dialogue, thus, is perceived by relativists and the antagonists of religion as a means to suppress different religions and ultimately establish a universal religion.

Religion is an essential aspect of individual and collective identity. It is particularly essential in the case of peoples and communities that live where past clashes or current conflicts are characterized by a religious dimension. The fundamental question is how to transform what could be a cause of friction into an asset for mutual understanding, harmony, and sustainable coexistence. Interfaith dialogue has the potential to significantly contribute to answering this intricate query while unveiling the richness of centuries, and at times millennia, of shared existence and reciprocal influence.

CHAPTER 15

Education and Peacebuilding

Unlike adult-led interventions, young people oftentimes construct an approach to peacebuilding that deemphasizes conflict escalation, which in turn influences the direction of local peacebuilding. For education initiatives as interventions to yield results, for example, promoting a culture of peace, investment is needed so that feedback loops inform further decisions. Choosing the path of education that reaches younger children serves the dual role of granting such talented young people an edge in life but also at the same time affords them the needed exposure and an opportunity for young people to participate in peacebuilding early in life. For Holdstock, in countries experiencing social unrest, conflict, or war, there are serious implications for the delivery of educational services. Often slow to develop and slow to realize in effect, the growth of a culture of peace, ethnic and racial tolerance and respect, equal opportunities, and gender equality are tenets of a democratic society, social justice, and identity.

Despite the "young" origins of youth peacebuilding, the knowledge and practice of youth-led initiatives has been increasingly recognized as essential channels to contribute to peace and investment in youth in particular. Youth leadership and engagement in peacebuilding is employed as a model of change through community empowerment, leadership and capacity development, and the creation of a non-hierarchical approach to problem-solving. There is situated in their ample time and flexible access to local communities which are beyond the reach of older age groups. This different approach to decision making emphasizes and makes available to the view alternative perspectives, experiences, and knowledge to inform policy development and implementation. For Paffenholz and Spurk, globally, working with young people to address social conflict has direct impacts on future negative conflict trends.

CHAPTER 16

The Role of Teachers in Connecting Cultures

The Role of Teachers and Students in Bringing Global Learning as Part of Global Education in Action. Teachers play roles as guides, mentors, and temporal and austerely advised taskmasters in the process of enabling students of all levels and ages to plan and think globally and act locally. They can teach students why and how all peoples on Earth are connected and about interwoven ways human actions and responsibilities are shared. Teachers can lead students as young as toddlers to think about positive changes they can make at home to live 3R practices. Co-curricular activities of doing, seeing, reviewing, researching, and writing about Litter or Water or Energy Reduction in daily lives at home should become routines of educational relevance. Tasks making recyclable bags, planting seeds, cutting and pasting of students' art unto class and home decorative components could be wondrous times of networking with students, just energizing schools and families in the most important 21st Century campaigns. Online support and collation of activities between students and schools should frequently take place.

The role of teachers should be affirmed and expanded both at home and abroad. Teachers are the hearts of every educational system. If you do not have good teachers, you are not really going to be necessarily successful in educating children. Teacher training is essential, including in building relationships with colleagues of different cultures. To expand relationships between the best teachers of different cultures, a Global Reach Out should empower teachers who have innovatively used internet and multimedia training tools to reach out and make a sustainable impact upon worldwide educational systems. The best Green Teachers who are educationists living and practicing 3R lifestyles should continue to be honored in an annual global Green World Teachers Week to motivate teachers diligently and consistently modeling Green Lifestyles for educational impact in home communities and students and teachers of other countries.

CHAPTER 17

Parental Involvement in Promoting Cultural Understanding

The national system of education, be it Romanian, Portuguese or from the other countries, should be run in accordance with this moral and human goal. At the same time, the national educational systems, we understand that in their life, as ours in the Romanian space, promote the idea of an alternative, balancing through multi-cultural training, education for identity promotion, based either on "humanistic" premises or on "nonhumanistic" premises, on so-called modernist cultural theories. These promote the educational principle of removing everything characteristic within a particular culture and accentuating the idea that a core values system should generate a single cultural reality above the major traditions.

As the mother and father help the child in the learning process, so should the teachers in the learning process of the child; and beyond the teachers, the teachers, the parents, are also to help educate the students in this era are young people about the universal values which foster international integration. The shared goal of the family and the school at promoting a balanced development of students presupposes the exchange of ideas and information being encouraged, dialogue being promoted with the many cultural influences and their creators, knowledge about the universal values and types of behavior being accumulated, our balanced approach as regards national and transnational, national and international dimensions being expanded. Cultural understanding in the positive sense does not mean generating international students, oriented in other circles, lacking national identity, rejecting the educational values characteristic to one or another nation promoting universal values in their desire to know, understand and receive the values of other cultures.

CHAPTER 18

Education for Global Citizenship

However, if global citizenship is the goal, what then is the role of education in achieving it? Traditionally, students are thought to be in the process of becoming prepared to take such a role through the careful transmission of values and the teaching skills they will need later. Education for global citizenship, in contrast, values the role of teachers and students as co-creators of knowledge. Knowledge is seen as something to be actively made, rather than simply transmitted from one person to another. In a world where the formulation and transmission of information and ideas are increasingly subject to control by small numbers of actors, often with particular interests, learning processes based on dialogue and sharing are particularly important components of global citizenship education. That is certainly a fact that various levels of education might seek to achieve.

What, then, is education for global citizenship? The starting point for any definition is the simple recognition that becoming a global citizen is a lifelong process. It is about becoming willing and able to live as a fully engaged and compassionate member of the local and global communities we all belong to. Such a person works with others to build relationships and institutions that are characterized by justice, compassion, and equity, relentlessly pursuing productive solutions to shared problems. As such, he or she is an active and responsible participant in a variety of communities, contributing to their well-being and affirming the dignity and rights of fellow humans. Importantly, in this definition, 'global citizenship' does not mean a person must be enrolled in academic study or be a holder of a particular passport. It is a call for all people everywhere to come together and work in solidarity to address our common challenges.

CHAPTER 19

Overcoming Language Barriers in Education

Dr. Garcia expresses his concern against contraction of opportunities for bilingual education amidst increasing power of English. I too recognized the importance of the Additive Bilingual model of language education and I have been doing research into it. The number of native language speakers in North America continues to increase, and at the same time the number of students in bilingual education decreases. People tend to form small communities with same language-speaking people and are afraid of surrounding themselves with people from other language background. Under these circumstances, Dr. Garcia has emphasized the significance of bilingual education as a human tradition. I myself have carried out research on this theme and have come to realize the ideal model of language education has unique value and is indispensable for the future of our society.

One of the pressing issues in education during our time is overcoming language barriers. The paper of Dr. Eugene Garcia, Professor of Education of Graduate School of Education, reminds us of an ideal model of language education. The Additive Bilingual Model was introduced in the 70s; it is a natural model of language education, in which a student's native language and English are supplemented both by language immersion. This model answered the need for students who did not have proficiency neither in the society's external language nor in their own native language despite the fact that their thoughts and emotions are expressed in their native language. They needed support from the society.

CHAPTER 20

The Influence of Education on Identity Formation

This is realized in the experiences of two countries, the Philippines and Hong Kong SAR. Both countries have a common interest in education and spirituality. These are not exclusive to Christians, but inclusive to people of all ages and religion as a yearning for peace and unity across cultures and peoples. Thus, the young generation becomes not only interested in making connections but also to develop a more profound spiritual learning. They long to grow deeper beyond denominational and religious affiliations, they yearn for deeper connections founded in the belief of genuine spiritual learning, dialogue, and education. With these in their hearts, the young men and women cannot do less but to respect and honor each person regardless of color, religion, or social status.

Education is important in a person's life since it is considered to play a crucial role in one's identity formation. If we were to consider this in the light of the teaching of Nostra Aetate, education through meaningful encounters can be a good medium in imparting to the youth important values in life. This echoes what St. Augustine said in his work Confessions, 'Teach me, O Lord, to do your will and your better not to engage my heart in fool's play. This inquiry of education as part of our own project becomes of greater significance when adopted as a pedagogical and spiritual response which may lead to genuine dialogue with our neighbors. It is in this light that the young individuals become more interested in engaging in life's deeper inquiries and aspirations.

CHAPTER 21

The Intersection of Education and Cultural Heritage

In light of the rapid expansion of globalization, there has been ample time for contemplations and discussions about dualities—greater interconnectedness leads to pragmatic loyalties, while it concurrently couples dispositions to the land. In turn, dual educations have emerged. These practices integrate instruction from a home-country, and the traditions that shape a cultural and ethnic identity, with those drawn from countries and populations in which endeavors and professions are pursued. The dual concept admits the idea of home and abroad that travels with an individual irrespective of the journey, and this is particularly important to address for those individuals who interact in the field of education.

This book, "Ties That Bind: A Handbook on Policies and Practices for Teacher Education," is a result of conversations and collaborations across cultures from around the world over a period of two years. Its goal is to inscribe in a tangible format educational practices to develop and open knowledge on cultural heritage for use in teaching and teacher preparation programs. It promotes mutual respect and an appreciation of inter- and intracultural references of the individuals that populate the planet we share, a theme that is of critical importance to humanity. More specifically, this publication seeks to grapple with the ways in which teacher education can be strengthened, allowing educators to undertake efforts to address unprecedented challenges as an international community.

CHAPTER 22

Education for Tolerance and Acceptance

Throughout history, understanding and accepting cultural diversity phenomena have caused people to follow different educational applications. One of these educational applications is curative programs aimed to eliminate the problems caused by cultural diversity. Another educational application is given in the form of developmental programs by which people's cognitive patterns are reshaped in order to understand cultural diversity. Pragmatic education presently carried out is closely interested in this second approach. It is important for the individuals within the society to realize the value existent in cultural diversity. Importance in understanding the values that the society offers is seen in that people are able to benefit from this situation. In this respect, being able to understand cultural diversity in society is related to understanding the value that people offer to each other.

Along with the principle of the acceptance of different beliefs and perspectives, understanding, containing, and appreciating people from different cultures is an important concept that should be taught to students through the education process. Understanding, containing, and appreciating people from different cultures can be provided with direct communication with the society, in service learning, and with the environment of different cultures in formal education. First experiences about cultural diversity are mostly gained through the family. The values adopted in the family, the knowledge of the society in which the family is situated, and the perceptions towards the society and the individuals are quite important in forming the perspective of children towards the culture.

CHAPTER 23

Multicultural Education and Curriculum Development

In today's multicultural society and environment, people need to understand their own cultural identities, but at the same time recognize and accept the identity and diversity of others; everyone should be able to coexist as equals and act with respect, courtesy, and consideration toward all others, regardless of cultural or ethnic background. Also, they argue for the use of multicultural education at two levels – within the classroom and the institution, which in this case of this university should be the department in charge of teaching teachers (for more details on the Y-TEC program, see the "Context and Participants" section).

There are many possible definitions of multicultural education. This chapter explains a useful framework: "Multicultural education is an approach to teaching and learning that is based upon democratic relationships and advocates cultural competence, prejudice reduction, and social justice and equal opportunity for all students." A culturally proficient person, continuing, "demonstrates attitudes and behaviors that promote effective and appropriate interactions in a variety of cultural contexts. Cultural proficiency assumes that individuals have learned to transcend their own biases, as well as grow their own resilience for bias episodic experiences."

CHAPTER 24

The Role of Arts and Culture in Connecting Cultures

Despite the mounting concerns regarding the role of arts and culture in the world at large, using them effectively to consistently bridge cultures all over the world is undoubtedly a challenging task. With the growing stress on education as a prime lever for establishing a peaceful global society, researchers, artists, and policymakers become more obliged to think about how to maximize the capability of arts and culture as instruments for motivating and nurturing international comprehension and mutual respect. Art can sensitize us to societal messages and connect our transcendental or individual experiences, endowing us with the touchstone for recognizing the universal messages from shared individual experiences that can connect individuals from diverse societies, thus bridging the gaps created by those who emphasize the differences.

In today's globalized society, arts and culture are not only instrumental in connecting all people, but also in connecting the different cultural and national interests, either through conflict or through unity. Arts can be one of the culturally specific and unique tools for communicating our traditions and from them, we are able to learn from other cultures. Since the Second World War, the aspect of observation for art and culture both nationally and internationally has emerged as an important dimension, whether in the aspect of an academic discipline such as international relations, overseas development aid, cultural diplomacy, community or organizational involvement, or individual enlightenment and entertainment.

CHAPTER 25

Education and Human Rights

Educating all citizens is key to building a culture of human rights that respects, honors, and truly embodies the principles to which most nations purport to ascribe. In emphasizing the key role of education in the promotion and protection of human rights, the International Declaration of Human Rights promotes "the development of respect for human rights and fundamental freedoms." Ushered as one of the first human rights covenants after the end of World War II, the Universal Declaration of Human Rights proposes that everyone has the right to a standard of living adequate for the health and well-being that should include "education." States, then, have not only an obligation to extend educational opportunities to all but a strategic one in that education can cultivate more respectful and inclusive human rights cultures dedicated to human, civil, political, socioeconomic, women's, labor, and cultural rights, among others.

Article 26 of the Universal Declaration of Human Rights states that "everyone has the right to education" and in the Millennium Development Goals, 1 and 2 focus on eradicating extreme hunger and poverty and achieving universal primary education. These societal aspirations reflect the critical nature that universal primary and secondary education have earned in making individuals, families, and communities healthier, wealthier, and more civil. Education, then, is more than an end to a means; not only an investment but a key instrument supporting international solutions to human suffering such as forced migration, poverty, and discrimination. Sacco and Simon suggest that fostering intergroup understanding, facilitating joint positive interaction, and igniting and sustaining intergroup cooperation and friendship are essential tools for peacebuilding.

CHAPTER 26

Promoting Social Justice through Education

Within the context of educational institutions, three main aspects: curriculum, methodologies, and the inclusion of knowledge or subjects in learning modules need to fit into the realization of the goals of social justice. This alignment is brought upon the cultural perspective of education that encompasses aspects of cultural diversity in all dimensions. According to UNESCO, Quality Learning which paves the way for social justice to happen should encompass four significant areas: providing cognitive flexibility, maintenance of cultural diversity, encouragement of a favorable environment, and exploitation of cultural treasures. These provide educated individuals that encompass diverse perspectives of thinking as well as broad varieties of solutions to solve societal problems. As an epitome of such openness, the students are expected to be able to learn from anyone, anywhere, which signifies the sure representation of the diversity factor in them.

"Our experience has shown that when education contributes to the poor becoming more aware of themselves and is conducted in communion with them and their surroundings, it can become a means of liberation from social conditions that hinder full human development," asserted Paul VI and further reiterated by his successors. This scenario closely resembles the concept of social justice which this dissertation endorses. Social justice can only be realized after the full development of an individual's human qualities and it is through education that such realization of human potentials could come to existence. Since society is an institution that is mostly run by people revolved around the cultural interactions among its communities, social justice reaches its goal and could be maximally served through the consequential exchange and appreciation of cultures, particularly cultural identities that are diverse and even in some cases could not be domesticated with one another.

The Challenges of Cross-Cultural Education

This chapter intends to present a challenge of obtaining cultural unity understanding. With the Stairway to Cultural Unity researched cumulative web information books, largely humanity unique for individual assessment and discussion involvement—clear directions, end instruction, policy, or plan for wide activity in education or life are not provided. Therefore, what is needed, based on current educational mnemonic devices, is an imaginative interactive use of the practical Stairway steps, seen as tools for learning organization in the acquisition of cultural soul-culture understanding. Since these ten brain/mind learning functions demonstrate the evolution of derivatives of defined abstract gene, e.g., The Algorithm Defined Gene Evolution of the Tenth Homo sapien Brain/Mind Learning Function, they can be presented in any sequence of reader/student choice; or if prepared, the ten functions line can be presented to students, examining the resulting personal and group learning thoughts in tree logic follows of a suitable number of generations of students at differing learning stages. To appreciate the vast brain/mind power generated with gene inheritance, one could involve a genealogy tree showing personal inherited abilities of friends, family, and worldwide inspiring individuals as to our current understanding of gene involvements.

Overcoming population and resource growth with the goal to preserve life on Earth requires acceptance of Homo sapiens as one human family of evolving brain/mind individuals. On this family foundation, basic education evolves into history-based wisdom, realizing our connections to the family of life on Earth—as well as our larger universe support system. However, an Earth history foundation has been neglected in education and is lacking in information tools of organization, evaluation, and final decisions necessary for understanding the weight of evidence required in evolving cultural diversity evolution, global culture unity, and personal life meanings.

CHAPTER 28

Education and Economic Development

Most economic theories start with some notion of utility maximization. In Economics: Principles and Applications, Marc Lieberman and Robert Hall present a two-part theory of utility based on the fact of incomplete human information and increasing opportunity costs. Contrary to most conventional economic theories, the authors derive educational investment as a consumption, not investment, choice. Conspicuously, knowledge is equated to education, and it is known that a nation's population can be educated in a lifetime, implying increased, not diminishing, investment returns. Education then positively contributes to economic growth through finance, innovation, human capital, institutional infrastructure, reduced fertility, and good health.

Among the numerous dimensions into which to organize our world are politics, economics, and culture. These dimensions defy separation, but their degree of distinction aids in understanding concepts, societal organization, and the interconnectedness of human experience. Adding to this separation, a globalizing world engenders deep, distinct thoughts about these overarching themes. The strong meanings tied to education's provision foster well-being without fail, with hopes of removing the vices of life: poverty, conflict, hopelessness, hunger, lack of access, powerlessness, and helplessness. This chapter explores the interconnectedness of education and economic development, describing three works that have made this connection presently without choosing one as an outcome criterion.

CHAPTER 29

Education as a Catalyst for Social Change

Bringing this down to earth happens to be the main function expected of the current educational enterprise aimed at directing our lives and existence to a morally saner, healthier, more productive, and spiritually grounded reality. On February 26, 2020, in the year "of God" according to our humble Eastern Ethiopian Calendar, Professor Akpan Hogan Ekpo, on the 2nd Michael I. Okpara Annual Lecture podium, spoke brilliantly on the theme "The Igbos and economic development in Nigeria: Lessons and challenges". He did not need to spend time on his introduction in Umuchinemere Pro-credit Micro Finance Bank Enugu. He is a regular from 1996. But then, as we say in Africa, "the tyranny of this morning does not topple the monarchy of yesterday". He reminded us when the seventh 2007 Pope Benedict XVI's Encyclical letter, "Spes Salvi", revisited spiritual and moral issues afresh, analyzing the difficulties affecting human hearts and grounds in Christian faith thus fields of spiritual energy, literally speaking, where this tremendous engine from the usage of man's freedom really operates. He spoke of values and the "values desert" that needed to be bridged. According to the good Professor, "... the main function of education (i.e., education at all levels) is to inculcate these values in the people so that the social construct is enriched and the outcome will reflect cohesion, not disintegration, peace, not violence, justice, not avarice and greed".

As the earth breathes under the weight of imposed inevitable organic isolation from the spread of the Covid-19 pandemic, we have since established – if we never knew before – that planetary relationships, as with all human relationships, are not built on one-offs but must be nurtured through constant communication and interaction. This has put into bold relief the necessity of education and scientific knowledge in all human relationships and engagements, discourse and exchanges – even for the divine relationship with the Almighty, we do need to learn, to "become wise and knowledgeable" (Ps 51.6) in His Creatures and Creation to adore Him better. The entire gamut of human engagements and even the creative self are a function of the dynamics of the human psyche sparked by technological advances and the information age, which coincidentally can only be the by-products of education and scientific knowledge. It is interesting that our brothers, the Jews, the ministers of the Jewish people, rabbis, and the like have come to respect addresses by scientists and other doctors of the sciences who bring in their comments and addresses to them the spirit of divine wisdom as expressed through events of a scientific reality within the realm of creation. As man moves towards loftier and greater heights of knowledge and understanding, he agrees more with the Creator of the Universe as he would also necessarily, to put it metaphorically, give his nod to the ever-revealed exhilarating beauty of His Daughter, Mother Earth. The inverse is also true. As Joseph Mayer summarizes in his gift of 1882, "The only legitimate and noble duty of the actual sciences must be reverence for the Creator, respect for His Creation, and gratitude through the knowledge of the same".

CHAPTER 30

The Future of Cross-Cultural Education

The convergence between today's interpersonal and inter-group communication processes and technology—a kind of future rapid prototyping that is brewing relationships to "we" greater than the ones occurring during periods when radio was the fastest communication technology—empowers an optimistic prediction about relationships across culturally different members in the future. In this socially connected education, cultural asynchronism as a teacher or learner is abolished for cross-fertilization; narratives of discrimination, judgments, value gaps, and even reductive descriptions impelling action against other cultural groups become rarer. It is a scenario that could lead to an "exportation" of attitudes to cultural differences that can impact cultural relations in other realms. To exemplify the expectations for this scenario, we discuss two theoretical concepts and present consumer-to-consumer relationships across cultural differences as an educational space.

Few educators questioned the need for education that fosters interconnectedness across the world's cultural and national boundaries. This educational system was designed to promote inter-group understanding, positive identity development, and social action. It would allow learners to construct meanings of diverse cultures and realize how they, as individuals and as members of diverse communities, can practice their capacity for mutually empowering relationships and shared leadership with people who are culturally different from themselves. It would provide learners with direct ways of "knowing human beings" so that they would contribute to making better friends and authentic colleagues. Unfortunately, cultural currents of oppression across the United States and the world counteracted the expansion of global education as policymakers took steps to defund, discourage, and discriminate against people of different histories and cultural features. This essay discusses this counteracting through the social psychological concept of denial used at either individual or societal levels.

CHAPTER 31

Conclusion

In conclusion, when we contemplate this multifaceted and complex subject of culture in all its paradox, steadic, dynamic, and change, it becomes obvious that what is behind this is actually our cultural and educational position as well, and what we project as our personality or our perceptive relations with the world in which we live. The main mammal which differentiates us from animal beings and other living things can be reduced to the intelligence which is actualized by perception, information, conception, insight, and consciousness, and plays a major role in shaping these values. Our perceptivities and approaches to the world we inhabit and our relations with what is around us are determined by our perception and understanding levels provided to us by our culture and education, and are not beyond our spiritual faculties (such as intuition, inspiration, and attitude) as compensation for our deficiencies. We should place great importance on education, our internal culturing, our enhancing wisdom capacities, and raising our consciousness levels to appreciate the beauty of the universe, bear witness to the advances in modern cognitive sciences and the developments experienced in the human adventure, and avoid the problems caused by humanity.

It appears to be clear that the issue of culture or aspects of culture is highly significant and dominant in its various forms, themes, and polarities. Education becomes a system of localization of all kinds of information, skills, and values in the process. Not just localizing, but affording us the readiness for action, as unimagined of the state has now become unsolvable for our existence because without that, we cannot survive. In other words, we as humans every time adapt and form the recognition of the education system. The main issue is our recognition in the education system, which the only thing that stands is culture.

www.ingramcontent.com/pod-product-compliance
Lightning Source LLC
Chambersburg PA
CBHW051455140726
47987CB00006B/2727